Little Pebble™

Construction Vehicles at Work

DUMPER TRUCKS

by Kathryn Clay

527 917 26 2

raintree
a Capstone company — publishers for children

Raintree is an imprint of Capstone Global Library Limited, a company incorporated in England and Wales having its registered office at 264 Banbury Road, Oxford, OX2 7DY – Registered company number: 6695582

www.raintree.co.uk
myorders@raintree.co.uk

ISBN 978 1 4747 2722 8 (hardback)
20 19 18 17 16
10 9 8 7 6 5 4 3 2 1

ISBN 978 1 4747 2726 6 (paperback)
21 20 19 18 17
10 9 8 7 6 5 4 3 2 1

British Library Cataloguing in Publication Data
A full catalogue record for this book is available from the British Library.

Editorial credits
Erika L. Shores, editor; Juliette Peters and Kayla Rossow, designers;
Eric Gohl, media researcher; Tori Abraham, production specialist

Photo credits
iStockphoto: amysuem, 19, kozmoat98, 5, 7; Shutterstock: Chris VanLennep Photo, 11, Faraways, 13, GIRODJL, cover, Johan Larson, 1, sondem, 17, TFoxFoto, 9, 15, Thomas Riggins, 21

Design elements: Shutterstock

Printed in India.

Contents

About dumper trucks 4

At work 16

Glossary 22
Find out more 23
Websites. 23
Index. 24

About dumper trucks

Look!

Here comes a dumper truck.

Count the big tyres.

This dumper truck has six.

See the dump box?

It holds the load.

dump box

Here is the back of
the dump box.
It is called the tailgate.

CONSTRUCTION VEHICLE

80

tailgate

The driver moves a lever.

Up goes the dump box.

The tailgate opens.

The soil falls out.

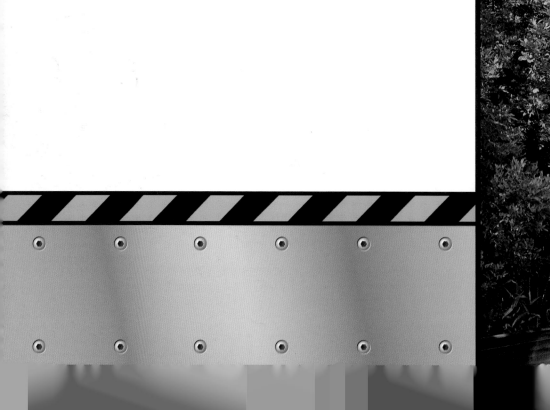

At work

Dumper trucks carry away big rocks.

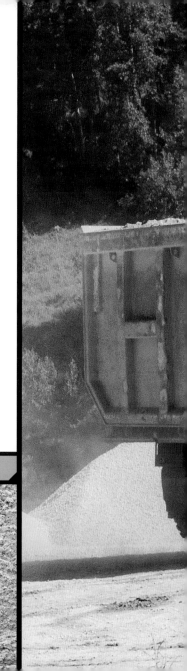

Dumper trucks bring
in gravel.
The gravel spills out.

Workers build a new road.

Well done, dumper truck!

Glossary

gravel loose rocks

lever bar inside the cab of a dumper truck that a driver uses to raise and lower the dump box

load what is carried by the dumper truck

tailgate part at the back of a truck that opens and closes

Find out more

Big Book of Big Machines (Usborne Big Books), Minna Lacey (Usborne Publishing, 2010)

Big Trucks (DK Readers Pre-Level 1), Deborah Lock (Dorling Kindersley, 2013)

First Book of Diggers and Dumpers (Bloomsbury Transport Collection), Isabel Thomas (A&C Black Childrens & Educational, 2014)

Websites

www.ivorgoodsite.org.uk/
Meet Ivor Goodsite, and learn all about safe construction sites.

www.toddlertube.co.uk/things-that-go/things-that-go-movies.html
The Things That Go! website has all kinds of videos about construction vehicles, including several videos showing dumper trucks at work.

Index

drivers 12

dump box 8, 10, 12

gravel 18

levers 12

loads 8

roads 20

rocks 16

soil 14

tailgate 10, 14

tyres 6

workers 20